"To have amassed great wealth and not return home is comparable to walking in magnificent clothes at night."

Taam Sze Pui, *My life and work, n.p. 1925, p.38.*

Chinese Voices *8*

Chinese Australian history as revealed by Chinese Australians themselves

From the "Piece of *8*" series of Chinese Australian History in 88 Objects

by

Michael Williams

Chinese Voices *8* - Chinese Australian history as revealed
by Chinese Australians themselves

First edition. January 5, 2025.
Copyright © 2025 Michael Williams.

ISBN: 978-1-7635605-5-0
Written by Michael Williams.

Published by: ChideStudy Press
For inquires or to order copies
Email: Chidestudypress@gmail.com
Website: chidestudypress.com.au

Cover design:
Stanley Hunt from *From Shekki to Sydney: An Autobiography*
Letter, Lau Gai Cheong to Tsun Kei, UNE Archives.
Wong Shee Ping, author of *The Poison of Polygamy*
Cover of *My Life and Work* by Taam Sze Pui
Cover of *The Chinese Question in Australia 1878-79*
Extract from Ang's defense, NSW SL.

Contents

Introduction

It has been said many times (by me anyway) that Chinese Australian history is perforce reliant on European observers – often of dubious quality and more often dubious perspectives (see *Observers 8*). Nevertheless, there are instances – increasing over time naturally – of Chinese Australians speaking in their own voice. Here are presented a selection of writings by Chinese Australian's in both Chinese and English. They range from the first (certainly the earliest extant) piece of Chinese writing in Australia as an indentured shepherd named Ang defends himself in 1850 from a murder charge, to a full novel written in Classical Chinese in 1910 on the eve of China's Republican revolution by the Melbourne based Wong Shee Ping. As well, there are reasoned attacks on discriminatory legislation, personal memoirs old and new, poetry, letters to those who have done well, and short stories expressing something of life in "white" Australia for someone of non-white heritage.

Together these 'Chinese 8' provide an insight into the many facets of Chinese Australian history as provided by Chinese Australian's themselves. Here they are presented in reverse chronological order – just for fun.

1. The Boy from Shekki

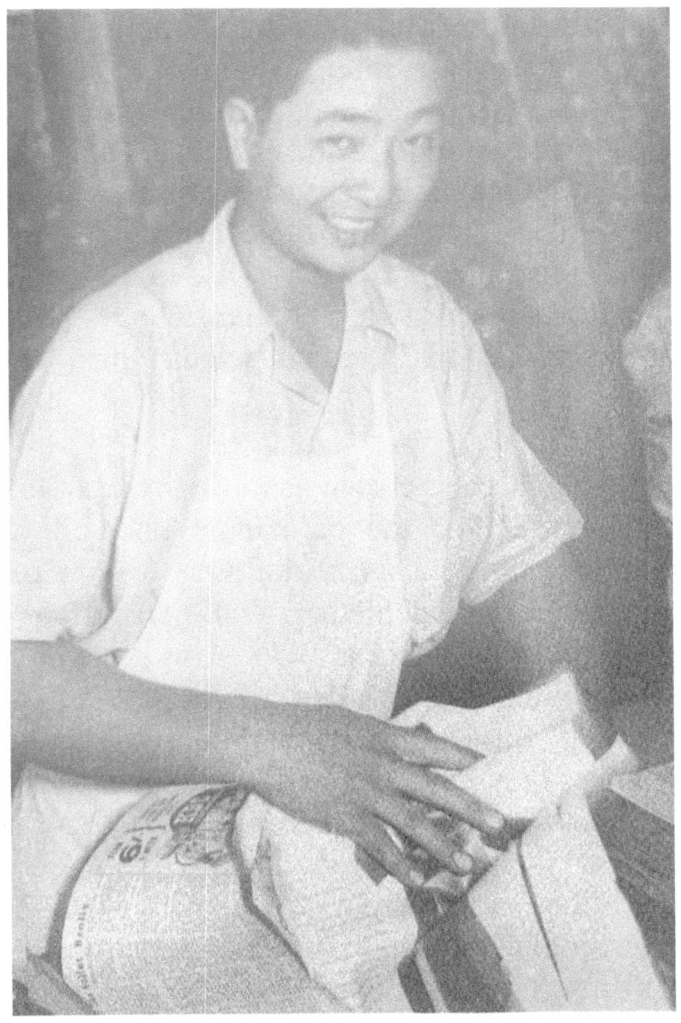

In many ways, the Stanley Hunt story told in *From Shekki to Sydney: An Autobiography* (wild peony, 2010) is a typical Australian one. Born in a south China village to a family with strong links to Australia and schooled in the county capital of Shekki, Stanley came to Australia at a young age and established his life here while maintaining ties with his home village. The most remarkable aspect of this typical Australian story — as typical as one originating in a British or Italian village — is that it is not generally recognised as typical.

Stanley Hunt can be seen as a bridge between the sojourner and the permanent resident, a dynamic that has been a defining feature of Chinese Australian history. For generations, fathers and grandfathers worked in Australia while maintaining families in China. Stanley embodied this Chinese-Australian heritage. Arriving at a young age, he largely grew up in Australia and worked in the vegetable trade for most of his life, a stereotypically "Chinese" occupation. However, as a store owner and employer of often non-Chinese staff, he did not fit neatly into many of the stereotypes of Chinese Australians that still persist. Later in life, Stanley was also prominent in Chinese Australian organisations and in donating educational resources to his family village in southern China.

Stanley Hunt's *From Shekki to Sydney* is one of only a small number of near-contemporary sources whose narrative stretches from the mid-twentieth-century wartime period through to the beginning of the twenty-first century. This remains a significantly under-researched period of Chinese Australian history.

Other works in this vein include Francis Lee's *Out of Bounds: Journey of a Migrant*, Andrew Kwok's *One Bright Moon*, and the excellent oral history collection by Mavis Gock Yen, *South Flows the Pearl*. [1] Together, these constitute invaluable source materials that greatly enrich our understanding of Australian history — sources that one hopes will continue to grow before living memory passes beyond our reach.

For more on Stanley Hunt see the Heritage Corridor:

https://heritagecorridor.org.au/mashan-village/

For more comments on *From Shekki to Sydney* see:

The Tiger's Mouth -
https://chineseaustralia.org/tag/shekki/

---

[1] Stanley Hunt, *From Shekki to Sydney: an autobiography* (Broadway, N.S.W.: Wild Peony, 2009); Francis Lee, *Out of bounds: journey of a migrant* (Petersham North, N.S.W.: Universe Books, 2010) and Andrew Kwong, *One Bright Moon* (HarperCollins AU, 2020).

Inside the blue covers of this intriguingly titled volume lies the first piece of Chinese-Australian literature written in English. It follows *The Poison of Polygamy* by some

13

twenty years and pre-dates the next example of this literature by nearly fifty. Why is this short story almost unknown, despite this distinction and its remarkable tale of a confrontation between a Chinese Australian and a European Australian in warlord-era China? The answer tells us something about the narrowness of perceptions of what is "Australian", as well as about the breadth of experience encompassed by the term "Chinese Australian".

The author, Vivian Yung Chow, was born and raised in Lismore, NSW, the son of a local businessman who had migrated from southern China and settled in the district. Vivian spent some years in Sydney in association with other local writers, contributing to a Sydney literary journal, *Readers and Writers Weekly*. However, like many Chinese Australians of his generation, he wished to contribute to China, which was undergoing profound change at the time. He and his brother therefore headed to Hong Kong and Shanghai, where their English skills and limited (or non-existent) Chinese allowed them to find work, usually with English-language newspapers.

This life story is remarkable only in how little most Australians recognise its typicality. The ongoing links of many Chinese Australians with the home villages of south China, as well as with the expanding and vibrant cities of Hong Kong and Shanghai — centres with a strong Cantonese presence — form a significant feature of Australian history. While increasingly well researched, these transnational connections remain largely outside popular understanding.[2]

Although the movements and China connections of these Australians are now better documented, the inner lives of Chinese Australians — often most vividly expressed in literature — remain comparatively unknown. For this reason, the recent translation of *The Poison of Polygamy*, with its dramatic narrative partly based on the author's family history, represents an important achievement. Twenty years later, the writing of the short story *What Happened to Riley* stands as another rare and valuable text in seeking to

---

[2] See Michael Williams, *Returning Home with Glory: Chinese Villagers Around the Pacific, 1849 to 1949*, Hong Kong: Hong Kong University Press, 2018 and Mavis Yen, *South Flows the Pearl*, Sydney University Press, 2022.

understand not merely what Chinese Australians did, but what they thought and felt.

While this is a work of fiction, there is little reason to doubt that some of the intensity of feeling and aspects of the protagonist's experience reflect the author's own. Without giving away the plot, something of the flavour of this Chinese-Australian perspective can be seen in the following passage:

> The world wants only one sort of Chinese. A humble, meek, ignorant fellow, soaked with opium and mad upon gambling. A clean-minded, clean-bodied, active-brained Chinese spells the doom of a white world dominion. And that, the white men have been clever enough to realise.[3]

Set in warlord-era China, this confrontation between two Australians of different heritages may unsettle some readers.

---

[3] Vivien Yung Chow, 'What happened to Riley' in *What happened to Riley and other stories: a selection of short stories by China's modern writers*, United China series no. 1, Shanghai, China: United China Publishing Syndicate, 1932, pp.169-170.

The full text of *What Happened to Riley* is available here.

The only public copy of the original publication is held in the State Library of NSW.[4]

For bringing this valuable work to light, Margaret Kelly, niece of Vivian Chow, deserves particular thanks.

---

[4] There it was originally catalogued as: "Short stories, Chinese — Translations into English & Short stories, English — Translations from Chinese." While the absence of any Australian attribution may be understandable, the designation "translations" appears to have resulted from stereotyping, as all the stories were written in English. The other three stories in the collection are also well worth reading.

Sydney's North Head Quarantine Station operated from the 1830s until 1984. During this period, passengers and crew from ships suspected of carrying contagious diseases were required to spend days, weeks, and sometimes months in isolation there. Many of these passengers and crew were Chinese and, like others confined at the station, often passed the time by carving their thoughts and feelings into the sandstone. The result is a rare collection of poems and inscriptions that offers a special instance of Chinese voices within Chinese Australian history.

The carvings are mostly difficult to read now and vary from simple names and dates to emotional poems and the occasional denunciation of imperialism or of Englishmen in general.

As soon as thinking of my younger brother without help.

I set off for gold mountain right away.

Occasionally a man died of smallpox.

He is a sailor on the ship.

Setting off and sailing to in the last month of the year.

By tenth of January next year, arrived at Sydney Harbour.

It is hard to say how much misfortune I have suffered.

I have been trapped and suffered from smallpox all these days.

Your advisable words are proved precious to me.

Nobody knows what trouble I am in.

I must not complain •••

Talking about it, I am surprised what I have done all these years.

I sincerely advise everyone should have his own decision.

The news that ten thousands Liang of gold buried in Australia spreads to China.

Lee Defang

An Englishman

Down with this type of man

This description of the St Albans carving was supplied to the Chinese Australian Historical Society in November 2015 by archaeologist Dr Peter Hobbins when he conducted a tour of the Quarantine Station:

A memento of the visit of the steamship *St Albans* in 1917 also reveals much about the Chinese history of Sydney's former Quarantine Station at North Head, near Manly. Created by layering concrete onto a sandstone cliff face, this inscription features messages in both English and Chinese. Latin characters were scored into the wet concrete to read simply "SS St Albans Feb 1917 SAH". For historians working in Australian and British sources, this is enough to track down Samuel Alfred ('Alf') Hollingsworth, third mate aboard the steamer when it was quarantined for smallpox over 16–19 February 1917.

© *Ursula K Frederick, Quarantine Project, 2014.*

As the limewash weathers after nearly a century of sea air, the panel is giving up another secret, and a more detailed message is emerging. Painted with a skilled hand, the Chinese characters has led to some confusion – particularly the somewhat cryptic column on the left. Speaking the characters aloud, however, reveals their intention: they sound out a close equivalent of 'St Albans'. The entire message has been translated to state:

"Erected in the sixth year of the
Republic, first month, twenty-fifth day,
to commemorate St Albans".

Who crafted this careful calligraphy — and whether they were permitted to do so — is unknown. Certainly, the *St Albans* had a mixed British and Chinese crew, and spent decades sailing between Australian and Asian ports. The symmetrical layout, which balances the English and Chinese messages may suggest that it was planned from the outset as a bilingual monument. Although the Chinese characters were later overpainted, an unintended benefit of this is that they have been better preserved as they reappear in the present.

Similarly, Chinese residents, travellers and crew caught up in quarantine have moved in and out of visibility at North Head since the 1850s. Across the landscape, they left over 100 inscriptions carved or painted onto cliffs, boulders, buildings and even drain covers, while others are memorialised in the nearby cemetery. Since 2013 a team of archaeologists and historians from the University of Sydney has been recording these inscriptions and seeking to tell some of their stories of travel, disease, internment, sadness and strength.

Stories from the Sandstone examines around 1,600 engravings in many different languages that were carved into the rocks and walls around the Quarantine Station over its 150-year history.

Peter Hobbins, Ursula K Frederick, Anne Clarke, *Stories from the sandstone : quarantine inscriptions from Australia's immigrant past* (Crows Nest, NSW : Arbon Publishing Pty Ltd., 2016)

4. "I heard you have been successful overseas."

Underpinning the sojourning enterprise that was central to Chinese Australian history for many generations was the sending of remittances. While with each remittance went always a letter. Yet relatively few of these letters have survived, and even fewer still are those letters from the recipients back to those who were abroad earning money.[5]

Translated here is an all too typical letter asking for money. It is one of many letters awaiting translation that are part of the wonderful Tet Fong collection. Originally from Tingha the letters are now in the Golden Threads Collection, UNE Archives, Armidale.

---

[5] For a comprehensive and fascinating account of the remittance system see: Gregor Benton and Hong Liu, *Dear China: Emigrant Letters and Remittances, 1820–1980* (University of California Press, 2018).

阿秀尊兄台鑒賀北念別後川來倏已多年毫芒音信

回歸邦於六月間踏圓邸五旋廈楳到表僑一九並

金佰壹拾式名堂媒衫勿掛懷內云此銀俾一本一刊開

拆財束弟一概代理拆要他財束請勿為念至

光兄諒有借銀手部於在仰　　兄不可失言為要祈

念　光兄往華有數拾年之天弟一方未有相會耳

今　光兄近六旬竟之覓他鄉未免逞步美望

光兄有些水腳銀即連旋家為上弟於旧歲冬月中

由南洋回家托賴身俸車安至亘同仔於旧年拾目

申完婚於三月旬邀遊外華責不盡云即請

財安

民國式年七月拾五號

弟廷鵬孝字

1-16

28

Lau Gai Cheong to Tsun Kei, no date.
Brother-in-law.

I heard you have been successful overseas. I am very comforted by that and I remember you in the past, from time to time you sent us some money to maintain us. We used the money to look after our old mother and for going to school, for marriage and for doing business. Now I have one son and one daughter and they have to depend on me. Unfortunately recently I have arthritis and every time I go to the doctor, there's no cure. So now I am working as a pedlar. The amount I receive is little but a lot of people depend on me (too many mouths to feed). This is not enough for my own mother, or to look after my wife, and I don't want to live and don't want to die either. Plus these disaster years we couldn't get any loans. Within the last two or three years I've given you two letters telling you about my unfortunate situation and asking you to give me one or two hundred dollars. It's just to cover some of our expenses.

Unfortunately I sent the letter like a bird flew away or a fish that swam away. One letter was returned to me and one has no received no reply. I have been waiting for a long, long time and this is a very sad situation. Now I wish to ask you for a little over a hundred dollars and send it to Heavenly Station so I can do my small business again. I may be able to make a bit of money and what I'm asking you is only a small fraction from what you have – 'just one piece of hair, you won't miss it much'. So I could at least know where my next meals come from and you will be blessed in your next life.

(There is a year but difficult to work out.)

Doris Yau-Chong Jones translator, from Janis Wilton's Golden Threads, UNE Archives.

Tet Fong himself worked as a herbalist in Tingha, NSW. He had four sons who ended up further south in Uralla. It is they who handed these letters to researcher Janis Wilton when their sister, Tet Fong's daughter Victoria died - they were in the Tingha house a block over from Wing Hing Long, now the Tingha Museum.

Tet Fong worked as a herbalist in Tingha, New South Wales. He had four sons who later settled further south in Uralla. It was they who passed these letters to researcher Janis Wilton after the death of their sister Victoria, Tet Fong's daughter. The letters had been preserved in the family home in Tingha, a block from Wing Hing Long, now the Tingha Museum.

5. The Poison of Polygamy - 多妻毒 A Social Novel - 社會 說

The first novel of the Chinese Australian experience was written before the fall of the Qing Empire, albeit by a die-hard republican. The rediscovery of this long-forgotten Chinese-language novel around a century after it first appeared in print offers a rare window into nineteenth century Australia from a local Chinese perspective. It also provides valuable insights into the emotional lives of the gold seekers and the wider social concerns of Chinese-Australians at the time of writing. More broadly, it is to be valued for offering a Chinese perspective on the experiences of migration itself and on the challenges of migration for families and communities.

Wong Shee Ping, the author of this highly entertaining read, serialised *The Poison of Polygamy* in Melbourne's *Chinese Times* newspaper, in roughly weekly installments, from June 1909 to December 1910.[6]

The novel is a morality tale that follows the highs and lows in the life of anti-hero Wong Sheung Hong, his virtuous wife, and the many characters he comes in contact with, during times spent in southern China, in south-eastern Australia and on journeys between the two. The story offers a dramatic and detailed account of Wong's humble beginnings, his not always moral efforts in life, and his eventual

---

[6] This article is a modified version of the historical introduction to *The Poison of Polygamy*, 'Why is Polygamy Poisonous?' by Mei-fen Kuo and Michael Williams, pp.11-35.

rise in prosperity in Australia before returning to his long-suffering wife in their home village.

Wong Shee Ping was the brother of the manager of the Pekin Café and the son of a gold digger and Melbourne businessman from the See Yap region of southern China. Written therefore by a direct descendant of a gold miner, *The Poison of Polygamy* presents a fictionalised view of Victoria's gold rush history. Like many works of fiction, it contains historical inaccuracies and anachronisms. Nevertheless, it provides rare insight into the Chinese experience and into community memory of that history. The novel is a document of its times and was created with a distinct political and social agenda to mobilise and shape Chinese Australian communities in ways favouring the revolutionary nationalist cause.

The novel tells the story of a typical divided-family of the mid-19th century. Histories of the males who moved often neglect the family's members, and especially the wives, who did not. *The Poison of Polygamy* is rare therefore in its focus on both the challenges male immigrants experienced in the Australia of that time, and on the implications of their departure for the families they left behind. Although much of the story highlights the importance of fraternity and clan ties for successful settlement in Australia, the novel also portrays a wife left behind in China who suffers from loneliness and sacrifices her life for the sake of the patriarchal family into which she married.[7]

The second half of the novel traces how arrivals from China transitioned from the tough life on the goldfields to becoming successful merchants engaged in trade between Australia and China. Still, their lives were complicated by traditional demands that they produce heirs to carry on the patrilineal family name. This often served as justification for polygamy, or acquiring secondary wives, a troublesome practice that often led to disharmony in the family – and which lends the novel its title.

The author, the novel, the newspaper, and the many readers who enjoyed *The Poison of Polygamy* when it first appeared in print all merit a place in the social, political and literary history of Australia.[8] This is a place long

---

[7] For a discussion of the women left behind see Michael Williams, 2021. "Holding Up Half the Family", *Journal of Chinese Overseas* 17.1, pp.179-195.
https://doi.org/10.1163/1793254812341438

[8] The many much shorter pieces of literature appearing in Australian's Chinese language press since the 1890s are well documented in Haizhi Luo, Towards a Modern Diasporic

denied not simply because the novel was written in Chinese but also because it was written in Literary Chinese, a form of writing that has now all but disappeared.[9] Even when such works have been translated, the translations often give the impression of a chunkiness or stiffness that the original does not deserve. *The Poison of Polygamy* and its new generation of English readers is extremely fortunate in being able to gain this glimpse into the world of pre-Republican China and of the Chinese diaspora in Australian. Not only as an historical and literary curiosity but in a rigorous but readable translation that allows the imagination and the drama of the story to be fully appreciated and enjoyed. This is an Australian story — one that all Australians can now enjoy and treasure, both those with and without Chinese ancestry.

Wong Shee Ping, *The Poison of Polygamy - A Social Novel*, translated by Ely Finch, and introduction by Mei-fen Kuo and Michael Williams (Sydney University Press, 2019).

Literary Tradition: The Evolution of Australian Chinese Language Fiction from 1894 to 1912 (Master diss., University of New South Wales, 2017).
[9] See Ely Finch's Translators Introduction in *The Poison of Polygamy* for a detailed explanation, pp.37-78.

閱歷遺訓

中華民國十四年

歲次乙丑

譚仕沛著

MY LIFE AND WORK

TAAM SZE PUI

1925

In recent times, a number of Chinese Australians have written their autobiographies, notably Stanley Hunt, Francis Lee, and most recently Andrew Kwong.[10] Ahead of them all, however, was the remarkable Taam Sze Pui, who published his short but striking account of his life as early as 1925 — and, for good measure, in a bilingual edition.

Few copies of *My Life and Work* now survive, though a digitised version leaves little excuse for not being familiar with this readable, valuable, and all-too-rare example of the voice of Chinese Australians in the late nineteenth and early twentieth centuries.

Like so many others, Taam Sze arrived in search of gold, and he quickly informs us just what a gamble this was:

> "There was a rumour then that gold had
> been discovered in a place called
> Cooktown and the source of which was
> inexhaustible and free for all. Without

---

[10] Stanley Hunt, *From Shekki to Sydney: an autobiography* (Broadway, N.S.W.: Wild Peony, 2009); Francis Lee, *Out of bounds: journey of a migrant* (Petersham North, N.S.W.: Universe Books, 2010) and Andrew Kwong, *One Bright Moon* (HarperCollins AU, 2020).

verifying the truth, my father planned to go with his two sons."[11]

In less than a month:

"Oh, what a disappointment when we learned that the rumour was unfounded and we were misled!"[12]

[11] Taam Sze Pui, *My life and work*, n.p. 1925, p.9.
[12] Taam Sze Pui, *My life and work*, n.p. 1925, p.10.

Taam Sze continues with his account of the desperate straits of the failed goldminers as they sought to earn money through vegetable gardening, domestic service – "disrespectful and the wages poor" – and restaurant work.[13]

Taam Sze and his brother did as many others did and worked at scrub-cutting — "saved by frugal living" — clearing land for European farming.[14] Eventually he moved into hawking and into business partnerships before setting up on his own.[15] Throughout his time in north Queensland, Taam Sze kept in touch with his relatives in China — his father had returned home — remitting money, contributing to funerals, and helping arrange family matters, including his brother's return to China and marriage (of whose intelligence he held a low opinion).[16] By 1892, Taam Sze also held a partnership in a Hong Kong store, which was essential in facilitating business transactions with southern China.[17]

[13] Taam Sze Pui, *My life and work*, n.p. 1925, pp.22-26.
[14] Taam Sze Pui, *My life and work*, n.p. 1925, pp.27-29.
[15] Taam Sze Pui, *My life and work*, n.p. 1925, pp.31-34.
[16] Taam Sze Pui, *My life and work*, n.p. 1925, pp.32-34, p.37.
[17] Taam Sze Pui, *My life and work*, n.p. 1925, p.37.

Taam Sze also touches on the central sojourner dilemma, one that led many to return repeatedly to their home villages and then back again to Australia. Money was to be earned in Australia, but, as the classical saying quoted by Taam Sze went:

> "To have amassed great wealth and not return home is comparable to walking in magnificent clothes at night."[18]

Taam Sze's solution was to remain in Australia and have a wife sent to him. This was the choice of a minority, for a variety of reasons, but with his parents already deceased, the principal impediment to this path did not exist in his case.[19] A family was thus established in Innisfail, and with children born, the family business flourished. Money, however, continued to be sent to China; property was purchased; and the children were sent on at least one visit.[20] In addition, Taam Sze helped others to migrate to Australia and find work, an essential feature of the chain migration that sustained the enduring links between Australia and southern China.[21]

---

[18] Taam Sze Pui, *My life and work*, n.p. 1925, p.38.
[19] Taam Sze Pui, *My life and work*, n.p. 1925, pp.39-40.
[20] Taam Sze Pui, *My life and work*, n.p. 1925, pp.41-43.
[21] Taam Sze Pui, *My life and work*, n.p. 1925, pp.43-45.

又值月之初一十五海潮當漲

察有將漫上埠情形　須預提防

遷貸樓上以避　免至臨事倉

皇無措　貸被水清　損失不堪

(八)戒感人以德　毋服人以力

禦人以口給　屢憎於人　舉凡

Do exert yourselves in that direction. The experience of the past serves as the guide for the future; if you do not know the hardship I have gone through, read the above pages. And if you want to perpetuate my work without laxity, observe the ten rules of business. Oh! Hing, Oh! Hing, carefully attend to all your affairs. Hereafter I retire with your mother.

TAAM SZ PUI

(*A native of Ny Chuen, Nam Hoi District Kwongtung, China*)

Written in my 71st. year
at Innistfail (formerly Johnson River), Queensland
February, 1925.

(59)

Taam Sze Pui's *My Life and Work* in its lovely bi-lingual edition provides in a remarkably concise manner all the elements of family, village links, poverty, remittances, business and hard work that are the core elements of Chinese Australian history in this period.

For a full version of *My Life and Work* **by Taam Sze Pui the National Library of Australia**

For a rare use of this source see: Sophie Loy-Wilson, A Chinese shopkeeper on the Atherton Tablelands: Tracing connections between regional Queensland and regional China in Taam Szu Pui's *My life and work. Queensland Review, 21*(2), 2014, pp.160-176.

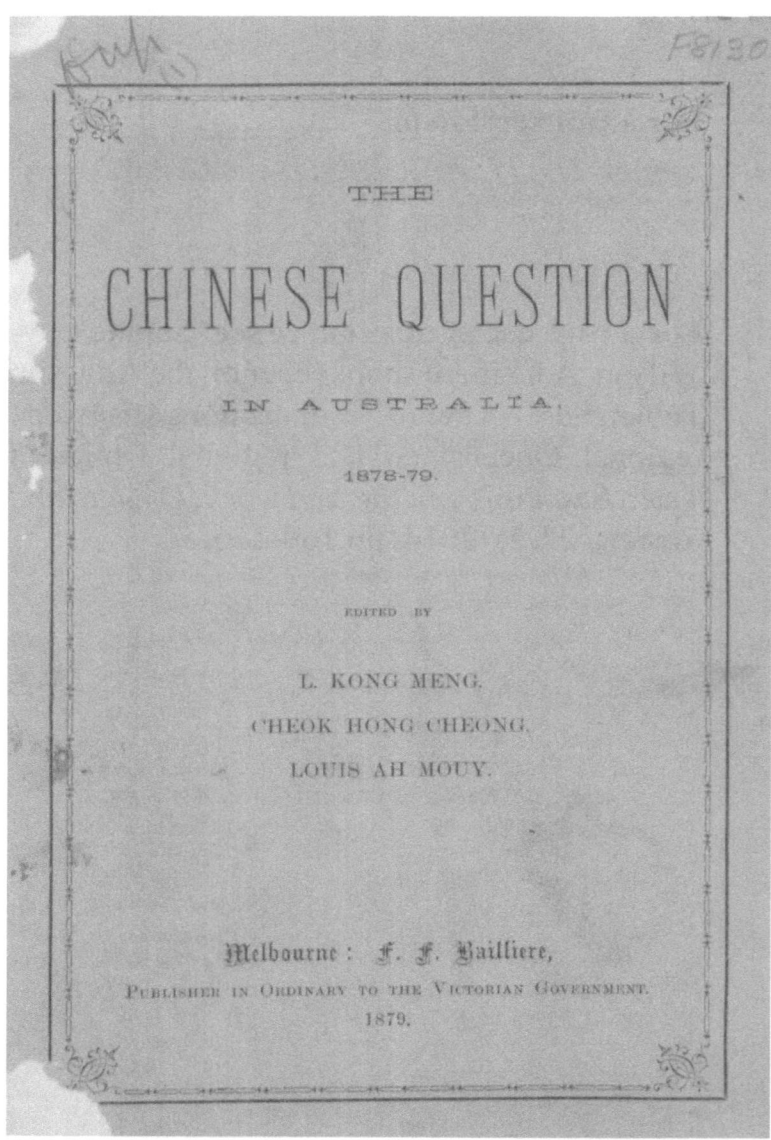

THE

CHINESE QUESTION

IN AUSTRALIA.

1878-79.

EDITED BY

L. KONG MENG.

CHEOK HONG CHEONG.

LOUIS AH MOUY.

Melbourne: F. F. Bailliere,
PUBLISHER IN ORDINARY TO THE VICTORIAN GOVERNMENT.
1879.

The presence of people from China in the Australian colonies was nearly always contested by those who arrived from, or were the descendants of those arrivals, from Britain. During the 1850s and 1860s this was particularly the case, as people competed for the lottery that was gold diggings. Violence and legal restrictions were both resorted to, and numerous petitions were written by Chinese people attempting to assert their rights and sway the governments of the day.[22]

By the late 1860s and into the 1870s the degree of conflict had lessened somewhat, only to begin to flare up again in 1878 — this time in relation to access to certain kinds of work rather than to the goldfields. The immediate response was a remarkable document written by three businessmen of Chinese heritage who had long been resident in the Colony of Victoria.

---

[22] See Anna Kyi, "'The most determined, sustained diggers' resistance campaign": Chinese protests against the Victorian Government's anti-Chinese legislation 1855-1862', *Provenance: The Journal of Public Record Office Victoria*, issue no. 8, 2009.

The Chinese Question in Australia 1878-79, edited by L. Kong Meng, Cheok Hong Cheong and Louis Ah Mouy is an effort to infuse rationality into an emotional debate:

> "… we appeal, as natives of China and as citizens of Victoria, to the reason, the justice, the right feeling, and the calm good sense of the British population of Australia".

On this basis it of course had little effect, and in fact the anti-Chinese movement would only increase from this point, culminating in the Immigration Restriction Act, 1901. Nevertheless, as the voice of those who had made Australia their home in defence of those of similar origin and aspirations, it is a remarkable document — comparable only to that by Walite Shah, written many years later.[23]

The very presence of Chinese people in Australia at all is laid squarely on the colonial power that had first violated the rights of the Qing government and demanded trade and freedom of movement ostensibly on a basis of equality. This argument is immediately followed up by an appeal to Christian-based

---

[23] See Debating White Australia

principles of the brotherhood of men. These are principles, it is further pointed out, that were violated in attacks on the Chinese gold diggers such as that at Buckland. It similar attacks had occurred in China itself, it is pointed out, this would have seen demands for "prompt reparation and adequate compensation" and, if such was not forthcoming, would have resulted in "some men-of-war" "ordered up to the mouth of the Pei-Ho".

NOTICE.

You are respectfully requested to circulate this Pamphlet amongst your friends, and thereby to assist the undersigned in their endeavour to give as much publicity as possible to their statement as to the primary cause of the immigration of Chinese subjects into these colonies, and as to their perfect right to settle in any part of the British Empire. If desired, more copies will be forwarded to you on application to the Publisher, or

L. KONG MENG,

CHEOK HONG CHEONG,

LOUIS AH MOUY,

CHINESE MERCHANTS OF MELBOURNE.

Having pointed out past hypocrisy, the current hypocrisy that inspired the document is arrived at. This is the proposition that Chinese seamen should be excluded from shipping in Australian waters. The hypocrisy of this proposition lying in the fact that a great deal of China's trade at the time was carried in English ships, with no likelihood that a ban on English seamen would be put in place.

> "Surely, justice is justice, right is right, and fair play is fair play, all the world over."

Many more arguments concerning misinterpretations of Chinese culture and government are put, as is a worker argument that betrays the class of the writers. The prejudice and hostility towards Chinese people in California is also discussed before the final argument that not to act with "reciprocity" can only bring great shame. A shame that the subsequent failure to act with reciprocity, despite the pleas in this pamphlet, present day Australians continue to deal with.

For the full text of this remarkable document, see the National Library of Australia

8. Case for the defence

In what is likely the first piece of Chinese Australian literature (broadly defined), a man accused of murder makes his defence. The accused, known as Ang, was from China and had been brought under contract through the port of Amoy (Xiamen). He was employed as a shepherd to replace convicts who were no longer available for such work. Not only did Ang not speak English, but from this defence — produced in a mixture of words and drawings — it would seem that his written Chinese or Fujianese was poor also. Nevertheless, his point was clear enough, as the accompanying note in English understood it:

> "This is the defence of a Chinaman accused of manslaughter. The Chinese characters are supposed to tell the same story as the sketches which evidently assert the death of the slain man to be accidental."

Now held in Sydney's <u>Mitchell Library</u>, the drawing is not among the surviving trial documents in the NSW State Archives. Rather, it was passed by mapmaker Frederick Proeschal to Justice Edward Wise, a progressive politician and Supreme Court judge who did not preside over Ang's trial (that was Justice Stephen). Wise deposited the document in the then NSW Public Library.

In addition to the dramatic images and faint pencilled text, we can now link this account to an 1850 incident and trial. A contemporary report observed that the drawing "may be found useful in eliciting the truth." We also now know that this same Ang was one of the two men on Cockatoo Island researched by Shirley Fitzgerald, concerning Ang's reluctance to leave before his mate Eu's sentence expired and their eventual pardon in 1853.[24]

The language and occupation of those depicted as shepherds identify the participants in this dispute and death as some of the many thousands of "Amoy" (really Fujian) people recruited as indentured workers into the Colony of NSW in the period after convict transportation ceased. These men are often forgotten by a history obsessed with the gold rush and the arrival of greater numbers of people from further south in China — Canton or Guangdong — and speaking other

---

[24] *Moreton Bay Courier*, 26 October 1850, p.3. See also Margaret Slocomb, *Among Australia's pioneers: Chinese indentured pastoral workers on the Northern Frontier 1848 to c.1880* (Balboa press, 2014) and Shirley Fitzgerald, *Red Tap Gold Scissors* (State Library of NSW Press, 1996). *[Thanks to Tony Anderson for pointing out the connection in the research of Margaret Solcomb.]*

languages. Nevertheless, many of the Amoy men remained and established families in Australia, and their descendants are only gradually rediscovering this ancestry.

The Amoy shepherds first began arriving in the Colony of NSW in 1848. While many later moved to the goldfields, others continued working in pastoral districts even after their contracts expired. Our defendant Ang was by no means the only Amoy man to appear before the courts. And there are numerous instances of court cases involving poor treatment or unpaid wages under the contracts on which men from Amoy had been brought to Australia. It was a tough life, and as one report observed at the time:

> "It is the intolerable cruelty that is exercised upon the Chinese labourers in this colony that causes them so very frequently to revolt and commit many outrages that might otherwise have been avoided."[25]

---

[25] 'Original Correspondence', *Bathurst Free Press and Mining Journal*, 12 August 1854 in Juanita Kwok, *The Chinese in Bathurst: Recovering Forgotten Histories*, Doctoral thesis, Charles Sturt University, Bathurst, 2018, p.71.

When Fujianese (aka Hokkien) speakers did appear in court, interpreters were frequently required. In the case of Ang, an interpreter had to be sent from Sydney before his trial in Brisbane could proceed. Although the drawing is not mentioned again in the depositions, Ang — charged with murder — was ultimately convicted of manslaughter and sentenced to five years' imprisonment. So perhaps his efforts to explain himself were "found useful in eliciting the truth."

For more on the Amoy Shepherds see:

Responses and Reactions to the Importation of Indentured Chinese Labourers by Maxine Darnell

Too Much like Englishmen by Michael Williams

Michael Williams is a graduate of the University of Hong Kong (HKU), a scholar of Chinese-Australian history and a founding member of the Chinese Australian Historical

Society. He is the author of *Returning Home with Glory*, HKU Press, 2018, which traces the history of peoples from south China's Pearl River Delta around the Pacific Ports of Sydney, Hawaii and San Francisco. Michael has taught at Beijing Foreign Studies University and Peking University and is a former Adjunct Professor at Western Sydney University. His website: *Chinese Australian History in 88 Objects* was shortlisted for the 2022 Premiers Digital History Prize and his most recent books include *Australia's Dictation Test: The Test it was a Crime to Fail*, Brill, 2021, *Every Requisite for a Campaign upon the Goldfields: Organisation, Victimisation and Mythmaking of the Walk from Robe*, ChideStudy Press, 2024 & *Too Much like Englishmen: Amoy Migrants in Australia*, ChideStudy Press, 2026. Michael is currently program manager of *Scattered Legacy* / 澳華僑海集珍, the national database of Chinese Australian history.

59

CEMETERY 8

WOMEN 8

MEMORIAL 8

NORTHERN TERRITORY 8

MUSEUM 8

NATIONAL ARCHIVE 8

STATUES 8

CHINATOWN 8 (MELBOURNE)

FAKES & MYTHS 8

TRANSLATIONS 8

CHINESE NEWSPAPER ARTICLES 8

LEGISLATIVE 8

APPRECIATION 8

PETITIONS 8

This material first appeared on the website - *Chinese Australian History in 88 Objects*

About *Chinese Australian History in 88 Objects*

This simple yet effective website showcases 88 objects from the history of the Chinese in Australia. It ranges over 200 years of migration history, illuminating political, social and economic aspects of the Chinese presence in the colonies and then Commonwealth. The objects come from both private and public institutions, each one including some discussion of its use and meaning in the past but also its curation and resonance today. Including bureaucratic forms and cafe menus, temple bells and even entire houses, this website provides readers with immediate access to a still overlooked part of the nation's formation.

The website is attractively designed and extremely easy to use — a reminder of the importance of thinking through universal accessibility to communicate with as wide an audience as possible. Its focus on the everyday stimulates users to think about the deeper histories and futures of other objects, both in Chinese–Australian history and in the history of other migrant groups. This beautiful portal promises only to grow richer as it finds more topics for investigation.

NSW Premiers Digital History Prize judge 2022

While there is much written on Chinese people in Australia, much of it is outdated or based on stereotypes. Over the last 20 years or so a great deal of new research has added significantly to our understanding of what is after all Australian history. However, there is still no one standard work that covers all of this history in any useful manner.

Listed below is a selection of excellent works which, together cover a broad range of this field. Any one of these well researched pieces will help you cut through the stereotypes that continue to predominate this history.

On women

Kate Bagnall, 'Rewriting the history of Chinese families in nineteenth-century Australia', *Australian Historical Studies*, vol. 42, no. 1, March 2011: pp.62–77.

On radicalism

Gregor Benton, "Australia", pp.72-91 in *Chinese Migrants and Internationalism: Forgotten Histories, 1917–1945* (Rutledge, 2007).

On the environment

Sheng Fei, "Environmental Experiences of Chinese People in the Mid-Nineteenth Century Australian Gold Rushes," *Global Environment*, 2011, 7/8: 111.

On politics

John Fitzgerald, *Big White Lie,* Sydney: UNSW Press, 2007.

On the North

Natalie Fong, The Significance of the Northern Territory in the Formulation of 'White Australia' Policies, 1880–1901, *Australian Historical Studies*, 49:4, 2018, pp.527-545.

On business

Peter Gibson, "Australia's Bankrupt Chinese Furniture Manufacturers, 1880–1930", *Australian Economic History Review*, 2018, 58: pp.87-107.

On merchants

Mei-fen Kuo, *Making Chinese Australia: Urban Elites, Newspapers and the Formation of Chinese Australian Identity, 1892–1912* (Clayton, Victoria: Monash University Publishing 2013).

On North Queensland

Cathie May, *Topsawyers: The Chinese in Cairns 1870–1920*, (Townsville: James Cook University Press, 1984).

On miners

Barry McGowan, "The Economics and Organisation of Chinese Mining in Colonial Australia", *Australian Economic History Review*, 2005, 45: pp.119-138.

On the villages of origin

Michael Williams, *Returning Home with Glory: Chinese Villagers around the Pacific, 1849 to 1949* (Hong Kong: Hong Kong University Press, 2018).

On coolie myths

Sophie Loy-Wilson, "Coolie alibis: Seizing gold from Chinese miners in New South Wales", *International Labor and Working Class History,* 2017, 91, pp.28-45.

On Chinese Australian literature

Wong Shee Ping, (Ely Finch, trans), *The Poison of Polygamy - A Social Novel*, University of Sydney Press, 2019.

On oral history

Mavis Yen, (Siaoman Yen & Richard Horsburgh, eds), *South Flows the Pearl,* (Sydney University Press, 2022).

On being a classic

C. F. Yong, *The New Gold Mountain: the Chinese in Australia, 1901-1921* (Richmond, S. Aust: Raphael Arts, 1977).

About ChideStudy Press

Michael Williams founded ChideStudy Press so that he could publish what he wanted as he wanted. An author of several academic works, Michael was dissatisfied at their high prices and lack of reach. Hopefully ChideStudy Press will change this.

Are readers stupid? Publishers seem to think so, with efforts to publish anything with footnotes or a close argument routinely refused. This leaves the so-called "academic" press which routinely refuses anything outside the favourite theme of the month, not to mention high prices and firewalls.

ChideStudy Press aims to publish cheaply anything of interest without much regard for popularity. ChideStudy Press aims to fill a "niche of necessity." Much of this history is buried in local archives, family stories, and bilingual records that traditional publishers often find "too difficult" or "too narrow" to market. This focus is on accessibility (low price) and depth (footnotes and close arguments), something the descendant community and serious researchers are looking for. ChideStudy Press publishes history mainly, and Chinese Australian history as a speciality, but you are welcome to suggest anything!

chidestudypress@gmail.com

Every Requisite for a Campaign upon the Gold-fields

Organisation, victimisation and mythmaking of the walk from Robe

Michael Williams

Of the many episodes that make up the oftentimes exotic impression of Chinese Australian history the 1850s walk from the small port of Robe in South Australia to the goldfields of Victoria has repeatedly taken on epic proportions. Its 'long march' like length, tales of hardship and death, not to mention present-day outrage at the discriminatory tax the walk was designed to avoid, all combine to make the stuff of legends.

Yet remarkably the telling of this history has largely been left to local historians with their characteristic eagerness to retell every tale and make use of every allusion to their subject with little regard to plausibility, contradiction or even relevance. Thus, while the arrival of thousands of gold seekers from southern China in the mid-1850s at Robetown on Guichen Bay, South Australia, in order to avoid taxes imposed by the neighbouring gold rich colony of Victoria is well known, it is surprisingly little understood in detail.

280 pages – Illustrated

To order via PayPal/Credit Card click here ($25)

To order as an eBook at Apple Books ($4.99)

To order by email click here ($25 – less for multiple copies)

Brief Sojourn in Your Native Land

Sydney's *huaqiao* and their links with south China

by

Michael Williams

Brief Sojourn in Your Native Land highlights the enduring connection between Sydney and South China from the late 19th century to the mid-20th century, maintained by thousands of Sydney residents born in the diverse districts of the Pearl River Delta. The work draws on a wide range of Immigration Restriction Act files, along with other sources such as the late 19th-century 'Royal Commission on Alleged Chinese Gambling,' the burial register of the Chinese section of Rookwood Cemetery, and oral histories from descendants of these residents. The narrative reveals the experiences of a generation often referred to as *huaqiao*, whose ties to their home villages are traced from youth through adulthood and into retirement, passing onto subsequent generations.

Key aspects of this enduring connection include the importance of their districts of origin, restricted marriage choices, evolving conditions in China, the emergence of a new generation, and the impact of the White Australia Policy's 1901 Immigration Restriction Act and its administration. Throughout their lives, the *huaqiao* were largely driven by a desire to support their families in their home villages, fostering ties between these villages and Sydney that lasted for at least two generations.

225 pages illustrated

Print Edition

To order on Amazon

Pay directly with PayPal

To order direct from ChideStudy Press - **$25** per copy (postage free) or two for $35

Epub edition $5

Too much like Englishmen

Amoy Migrants in Australia

不屈從認命的廈門仔

By Michael Williams

Too much like Englishmen uncovers a forgotten migration that reshaped colonial Australia long before the gold rushes made Chinese migration visible. Between 1848 and 1853, more than 3,000 men from Amoy—modern Xiamen in China's Fujian province—were recruited under five-year labour contracts and sent to New South Wales. Drawn into the expanding British imperial labour market after the First Opium War opened Amoy as a treaty port, these men were dispatched to the pastoral frontier, where they worked as shepherds on remote stations struggling to replace convict labour.

Their recruitment was often opaque and coercive, their voyages arduous, and their lives in Australia profoundly disparate. Some endured exploitation, isolation, and violence; others resisted mistreatment, adapted to new conditions, and forged lives beyond the terms of their contracts. Tensions surrounding abusive recruitment practices erupted in the Amoy riots of 1852, abruptly ending organised labour migration from the port to Australia.

When their contracts expired, these men did not simply vanish from history. Some moved on to the goldfields, but many remained in rural Australia, marrying locally, becoming naturalized, and establishing families whose descendants live in Australia today. Long eclipsed by later Cantonese migration and distorted by the enduring stereotype of "coolie" labour, their experiences have been marginalised or misunderstood. Drawing on newly uncovered archival records and family histories, *Too much like Englishmen* restores these men to the centre of Australia's colonial story, revealing a complex history of resilience, agency, and belonging.

$5 (downloadable EBook only)

Free if you are a descendant of an Amoy man

To Order directly from ChideStudy Press click here

To buy via PayPal click here

Also available at Booktopia

Observers *8*

European Australian observations
on
Chinese Australians

From the "Piece of 8" series
of
Chinese Australian History in 88 Objects

Michael Williams

Having read what Chinese Australian's had to say about Chinese Australians now is your chance to read what European Australian had to say about them.

The selections range from the comments of a naive English teacher to those of an experienced China consul. From eyewitness to the arrival of the first 150 Chinese gold seekers to pass through Bathurst in 1855, as well as the astonished spectator to a Chinese opera. Not to mention the creations of the authors of both *Mary Poppins* and *The Man from Snowy River*. Of course, these selections would not be complete with reports from one each of those instant experts – the journalist and the travel writer.

Together these 'Observers 8' provide a fascinating insight into some of the many facets of Chinese Australian history.

Contents

No. 1: *My Chinese* by Margaret Egerton

No. 2: The Man from Shanghae, J. Dundas Crawford

No. 3: Amazing the yokels of Bathurst

No. 4: A Night at the Opera

No. 5: Ah Wong meets Mary Poppins

No. 6: A white women in Chinatown

No. 7: To the goldfields by Omnibus

No. 8: Jimmy the Pat

To Order directly from ChideStudy Press click here **($5 plus P&H)**